Please Feed the Macaws...
I'm Feeling Too Indolent

Also by Kevin Densley and published by Ginninderra Press
Vigorous Vernacular (Picaro Press)
Lionheart Summer (Picaro Press)
Orpheus in the Undershirt
Sacredly Profane

Kevin Densley

Please Feed the Macaws...
I'm Feeling Too Indolent

Acknowledgements

Poems in this book previously appeared, sometimes in slightly different form, in the following publications (Australian unless stated otherwise): *Burrow, Nightingale and Sparrow* (USA), *Platform, Quadrant, Sage Cigarettes* (USA), *Sudo* and *The Footy Almanac*.

Please Feed the Macaws…I'm Feeling Too Indolent
ISBN 978 1 76109 616 7
Copyright © text Kevin Densley 2023
Cover image: *Twilight on the Terrace, Paris* by Julius LeBlanc Stewart

First published 2023 by
GINNINDERRA PRESS
PO Box 3461 Port Adelaide 5015
www.ginninderrapress.com.au

Contents

Paris, 1877	7
Sylvia and the Lorelei	8
Rewriting, Reliving	9
A Change in the Atmosphere	10
Propinquity	12
Renaissance Scene	13
Hooray for Hollywood	14
Two Portraits	15
Imponderables	16
Kate Kelly (1863–1898)	17
Basketball	18
On William Hogarth's *The Graham Children* (1742)	19
Once a Catholic…	20
Italicised Poem	21
Mister Vernacular	22
Five Miles from…	23
Three Bushranger Trials in Berrima…	24
Jack-o'-lantern	25
Definition	26
Measures Taken	27
Sickle Moon	28
Revelations	29
Self-portrait as a Violin Belonging to Anne-Sophie Mutter	30
Manly Ferry in Thunderstorm	31
Rat Sonnet	32
Proximity	33
Tripedal	34
In Memoriam	35
Jaded Shakespearean Actor	36
Trapped	37

Youthful, Secret Desire to Have Sex…	38
That Thunderclap Blow	39
The Cowardly Captain Speaks	40
As Happy as Larry	41
This One, For Example	42
mr balloonman likes little children	43
In the Heartland	44
The Musician and the Boy	45
Dying Thoughts of Dr Josef Mengele…	46
Venticelli	47
Sitting on my Back Veranda…	48
Remembrance of Cigarettes Past	49
Get Me My Cloak and Staff!	50
Harlequin	51
Ghost Train	52
Night Journey	53
The Best Times	54
John 18:10–11	55
Joseph of Arimathea	56
Thailand Silk	57
Murray Cod	58
Goodbye Georgie	59
Resumé	60
Zombies	61
Nineteenth Century Street Scene: Evening	62
Contemplation upon the Death Mask of Alban Berg…	63
The End	64

Paris, 1877

after Twilight on the Terrace, Paris, by Julius LeBlanc Stewart

'Please feed the macaws,'
she said to me,
while reclining on her chaise longue.
'I'm feeling too indolent.'
We were on a wide stone balcony,
overlooking the City of Love.
She fluttered a pale hand
towards a pair of brightly plumed
– crimson, yellow and cobalt blue –
South American parrots
clamouring for attention.
I went to get the sunflower seed
but when I returned
both she and the birds
had disappeared, been carried away
upon the zephyrean air.
Sadly, I plucked a lament
on the dulcimer left lying there,
one from the Abyssinia
of our journeys an aeon ago.

Sylvia and the Lorelei

Sylvia walks a narrow path
through a forest of tall trees,
drawn by voices calling her
from the fathomless depths
of the freezing river,
the voices of maidens
with long, flowing,
marble-heavy hair.
Pinned to the sky
is a Gothic moon,
which Sylvia barely notices
as, entranced by the voices,
she advances;
a voluptuous virgin chorus
is calling her,
calling her,
calling to her
as they rise through the twilit deep.
She's a slave to their siren song
as they sing
that this is a night to drown in.

Rewriting, Reliving

Rewriting an early poem
– because you like it so much
but can now see the faults,
not obvious then –
is like trying to relive youthful days
with the benefit of experience;
you make the effort, kidding yourself
that, with what you know now,
the result will be wonderful:
you won't make the same mistakes twice.
But every time you try
to rewrite, relive the past,
you see no other outcome
was ever possible
than what you did then; it is
utterly of its time.
Rewriting, reliving the past ensures
only two guarantees:
disintegration and failure.

A Change in the Atmosphere

I feel it —
there's something
evil
around here;
it's almost
palpable,
the air
has suddenly
gone cold;
a strange
foul odour
wafts under
my nose;
dank spiritous
mists rise
from the ground,
transude
through the bark
of trees.
I sense
the presence
of ill-will
close by.
Somebody
near
has malevolent
intent
— *I can feel it.*

Or is it to do with
this still winter's night,
the wild dogs howling
in the nearby forest
and the fullness of the dreamy yellow moon?
Perhaps it's simply
my imagination.
What do you think,
my pale, hooded companion,
half-smiling
Nosferatu?

Propinquity

Curled up dogs – plaster cast –
entwined lovers
wrought similarly;
pots and drinking vessels;
murals on the walls;
eternally halted attitudes
of flight, of passive acceptance,
mark Pompeii's inclusion
in the annals of history.
But the same Vesuvian fate befell
nearby Herculaneum,
Stabiae, Oplontis,
Boscoriale
– Pompeii's lesser known
little sisters-in-tragedy.

Renaissance Scene

The pretty duchess
leads a brace
of whippets
skitter-clatter
across a tiled portico.

Hooray for Hollywood

High in the Hollywood Hills,
the cadaverous and the mummified
– B-grade movie actors
of the sixties,
television sex symbols
of the seventies and eighties
– haunt minor mansions
among braces of toy poodles,
pomeranians, shih tzu,
summoning illegal Mexican
waiting staff, pool cleaners,
occasional semi-literate
gym-bodied young men or women
who want to be in pictures.

These stars of decades past
leave their houses rarely,
to be the Marshal of their hometown fair
in small Midwestern or Southern towns,
sitting on a throne
in the lead float of a street parade,
waving at happy people,
some of whom remember who they were
– or else they go to conventions,
signing memorabilia,
people's arms (and sometimes breasts)
in exchange for clutches
of dirty green bills.

Two Portraits

for CRL
after Joni Mitchell, 'Woodstock'

Jesus Christ in the Summer of Love

Gazing directly from the frame,
solemn-serious is your father,
a beautifully groomed, yet hippy Christ
directly from the Summer of Love.
You, chubby baby,
seated on his lap,
reflect his expression,
held in thrall
by a father's God-like aura.

Earth Mother, White Witch

Nearby, the photo
of you and your mother
is of the same time,
identically posed,
but she is no Christian figure; instead,
an Earth Mother exuding love,
long wavy dark hair, smiling sweetly,
White Witch brimming with happy spells,
summery in calico.
Both yours and Mum's faces reveal the same thing:
contentment, serenity.

Imponderables

Where do birds go
when it gets dark?

Why do people look
into their handkerchiefs
after blowing their nose?

When the Loch Ness monster
is patently a fiction,
how come all those expeditions?

And why does a piece of buttered toast
always land face down?

Kate Kelly (1863–1898)

After 'the outbreak' was over –
two brothers dead,
her mother
and another brother
in and out of jail –
she moved to New South Wales,
married, had six kids,
and was found floating
face down in a lagoon
in the backwaters of the Lachlan,
while still in her mid-thirties.

What a colossal shit it can be
when other members of the family
become notorious household names.

Basketball

Hairy, sweaty underarms.
Echoing tin-roofed sheds.
Loud voices, leather balls
hammering off lacquered floors
and polished glass backboards.
Game for stupid
motherfuckers.

On William Hogarth's *The Graham Children* (1742)

In the background, the eyes of the family cat glare
scaring a caged bird.
Note the clock on the left,
surmounted by Cupid wielding a scythe,
suggesting that childhood is short;
then, there's the boy on the right
happily playing with his music box,
apparently believing the bird
is singing along with his joyful tune
when instead its song is one of terror
at the nearby cat.
And Daniel Graham's four children
look to have stepped into light
ahead of enveloping gloom.

Once a Catholic…

This morning, at breakfast,
I drank
Twining's Afternoon Tea.

I feel a little guilty.

Italicised Poem

Don't you think
italicising words
in a poem
often makes what is said seem
more intelligent
and significant
than it actually is?

Mister Vernacular

talked like a butcher's magpie
covered more ground than the early explorers
was as ugly as the old man's backside
gave me a father of a hiding
made the greatest comeback since Lazarus
was as graceful as a cow with a cup of tea
mad as a cut snake
often Molly the Monk
sometimes happy as Larry
toey as a Roman sandal
made silk purses out of sow's ears
had a beer pocket but a champagne purse
didn't know whether he was Arthur or Martha
went from chocolates to boiled lollies
had an eye like a mullet that stunk
– I mean a stinking mullet.

Five Miles from…

The dog sat on the tucker box:
'sat', perhaps, a euphemism
for the bodily function
this iconic canine performed.

Three Bushranger Trials in Berrima, New South Wales, September 1841

There is, sometimes,
a lack of light…

Paddy Curran, tried
for rape and murder.
Found guilty.
Sentence – death.

James Berry.
Guilty of murder.
Death.

John Wright.
Murder.
Death.
After his sentence was passed
the judge extended
no hope of mercy.

Wright thanked His Honour
then coolly asked
if he might have a candle,
as his cell was very dark.

Jack-o'-lantern

Jack-o'-lantern,
hideous pumpkin,
sinister grinner,
country bumpkin,

all the long year
you're a sight unseen
until you startle
at Halloween.

Definition

'Rival poet':
lacking-in-talent bastard
with undeserved success.

Measures Taken

Walking four miles near midnight
to save the taxi fare.

Playing a five-string guitar.

Kicking a newspaper football
tied into shape with string.

Selling the childhood coin collection
to pay an extended telephone bill.

Improvisations upon a theme…

Sickle Moon

Sickle moon,
the light you send
is watery-thin,
weak as piss.
You're a sick old man
with a prostate problem
who has to shake it out in dribbles;
unable to perform his task
with the effortless ease of former times.
I gaze into the night, depressed.
What a poor excuse for illumination!
When I want light
all you can give
is a dismal, far-off glimmer.
Invalid pensioner
in the depths of winter,
rheumy melancholic
in a larder dark and bare,
your days of full-bloom health
are far behind you
– aren't they, sick old man?
You'll fade away to nothing soon.
We both know it, don't we,
sick and sallow,
wrecked and weary,
dilute, dreary,
sickle moon?

Revelations

Christ the Leopard
coughs in the maze garden

Holy Mother forgive me –

Billy Bunter
farts in the greenhouse

*lately there has been a distinct falling of
in the interest given to hunger artists*

Holy Mother forgive me –

'S wonderful 's marvellous
PATRONS: DO NOT FEED B. BUNTER

Holy Mother forgive me –

The Lion and the Bicorn
decline to trot, but canter

Holy Mother please fucking forgive me –

Up and down and
left to right we wander

Please forgive me –

Self-portrait as a Violin Belonging to Anne-Sophie Mutter

Few feelings in life are as divine
as her beautiful hands moving closer.
I know I could never decline
the touch of this *virtuosa*.

Manly Ferry in Thunderstorm

Skies grimmest
dark lead.

Lashing rain
on white-capped Sydney Harbour.

Fork lightning spikes,
electrifies
the desolate arc.

Black thunder unfurls, reverberates.

The ferry creaks and pitches. Inside,
I fix my eyes on land, afraid,
silently praying for refuge.

Rat Sonnet

There
they
scuttle,

along
the
fencetop,

descended
from
the tree,

pink and white flowers
delicately
between
yellow
teeth.

Proximity

In the mid nineteen-thirties, my grandmother often made the four-hour journey to visit her older sister. She'd stay overnight, and many times was kept awake by roaring lions, bored and restless beneath the stars.

She could feel them very close, imagined all she had to do was open the bedroom curtains a little and there one would be, on the other side of the glass, staring back, eyes blazing. On second glance – in her imagination – this solitary lion seemed more quizzical than threatening, as if simply curious about the light in her room while the world about her slept.

But she wasn't on a reservation in the dark heart of Africa, or even in a village on the edge of savanna; she was in a house in Parkville, Melbourne, and her sister lived near the zoo.

Tripedal

Walking along the street,
I saw a three-legged cat.
Walking along a bit further,
I saw a three-legged dog.
What does this signify?

Mutant local life forms?

A deviant with a cleaver?

In Memoriam

A well-known poet recently died.
Many of his poet-friends
are falling over each other to write
memorial pieces for inclusion
in newspapers, journals and magazines,
equally for self-promotion
as in his memory.

Me? I couldn't stand the prick.

Jaded Shakespearean Actor

I am bound upon a wheel of fire
blah blah blah…

Is this a dagger I see before me?
blah blah blah…

To be or not to be
blah blah blah blah blah…

Trapped

Isn't it terrible
when, at a party,
you're introduced by a friend
to someone vaguely familiar
and you feel compelled to like the person
because of the introducer,
yet all through the evening
you're uneasy when that person's around,
then, just before you leave,
the realisation's suddenly clear
that they're someone from your distant past
whom you loathed at first sight
and, more than this,
the feeling was reciprocal?

Youthful, Secret Desire to Have Sex with the Long-dead Biographical Subject

I could have saved her life.
She wouldn't have died of TB
if I was on the scene.
I'd have taken her to a sunny clime
much earlier
and nursed her back to robust health.
With me, she would have blossomed:
Miss Socially Stunted, Inhibited
who only expressed her passion
through the written word
would not have been.
I'm sure we'd have enjoyed
wild, wonderful sex.
With my support, she could have fulfilled
her every talent and dream.

Who am I kidding?

That Thunderclap Blow

You never know when it could happen,
that thunderclap blow
– a heart attack,
a massive stroke…
One minute, you're here.
Next,

you're gone.

The Cowardly Captain Speaks

Fearful, I deserted the ship
but it wasn't sinking
– it only went down
after I leapt overboard.

As Happy as Larry

I'm not as joyful as Harvey
but more buoyant than Tom,
though I would be content
with the plain happiness
of my good friend Laurence.

This One, For Example

Certain poems behave
like a magical snake
which coils upon itself
then disappears up its own arse…

mr balloonman likes little children

look at mr balloonman
weeeeeeeeeeeeeeeeeeeee!
look at him,
the balloonman
weeeeeeeeeeeeeeeeeeeee!
balloons red and orange
weeeeeeeeeeeeeeeeeeeee!
we little children
laugh and leap
and gatherroundhim
weeeeeeeeeeeeeeeeeeeee!
we all cry
weeeeeeeeeeeeeeeeeeeee!
we are so happy!
we have smiles on our little faces
and glints in our little eyes!
happy are we little children
with kindlyold mr balloonman
happy are we so happy are we
we have sharp pins
to burst his fucking balloons.

In the Heartland

Somewhere in Iowa,
during the '92 American
presidential campaign,
then-President George Bush Senior
was 'mooned' by a family of five
as he chugged by on his train
full of organisers, media and hangers-on.
Yes, five bare arses
of various sizes
gave him an opinion
of his performance over the past four years.
A couple of days later,
still on his whistle-stop tour,
a journalist asked him, late in the evening,
'How was your day today,
Mr President?'
George Bush laughed and shook his head.
'Well, Roger, it musta been OK,' he joked.
'I only got mooned once!'

The Musician and the Boy

Julian played the bass trombone
in our school band
but he never practised,
his musicianship was questionable
and, anyway,
the instrument was a joke.
The notes he blasted
sounded like a quacking duck.
I remember a competition
where Julian played
'The Great Salvation'.
We boys renamed it,
after hearing his rendition,
'The Great Masturbation'.
But no one laughed louder than Julian
– he had a sense of humour
and couldn't have cared less.

Dying Thoughts of Dr Josef Mengele, while Having a Stroke and Drowning off the Coast of Bertioga, São Paulo, Brazil, 7 February 1979

When you're drowning,
the water
bubbles above you,
through the translucence
to the undulate surface.
Beyond is the sky,
azure today.
The sun is a disk
of hammered, hot gold.

My head's in a vice.
My right side is numb.
I sink fast. I know
there is no way back.
I fade, yet I remember
those eyes,
the eyes
of terrified children.

But it was my work,
and I am not sorry.

Venticelli

They enter through spaces
under doors,
sneak between slatted air vents,
high on walls,
come in when windows
are left ajar,
these little winds.

Sitting on my Back Veranda on a Late September Evening

Spring is whispering 'Summer.'
The chill has left the air,
gone for half a year
till melancholy autumn,
once more, murmurs
'Winter.'

Remembrance of Cigarettes Past

Craven A…
Camel…
Turf…
Where have all the lung-busters gone?
What of those craggy figures
who stood in front of TABs
coughing up their guts?
Too many anti-cancer ads,
tidal waves of health
have swept their kind away.
Oh for that glorious golden age
when smokers *felt* their cigarettes
doing real and instant damage.

Get Me My Cloak and Staff!

Animals love me
like St Francis of Assisi.
Twittering, brightly coloured birds
flutter about my head when I walk,
nest in my hair.
Cats leap onto my lap
to be tickled.
Dogs leave their owners and bound to me,
wanting to play ball.
I don't know why
I've been blessed with this gift.
I should use it more.

Harlequin

'Art is a lie through which we see the truth.' – Picasso

In 1906,
a young Andalusian painter
shipped himself to Melbourne,
attended a training session
of the Carlton Football Club
and painted a picture
of what he saw,
a now-lost early work
of a clown in multicoloured clothes
clutching a balloon
of inflated leather.
Other clowns
in similar garb
danced behind him
on a green field.

Ghost Train

at the Geelong Show, when I was a child

Luminous,
with a guttural roar,
the creature leapt from the dark.
My heart almost jumped from my throat.
But a kid at the back
of the Ghost Train,
in the carriage behind mine,
attacked the humanoid being
with, upon a closer look,
suspicious rubbery skin.
There was a struggle.
During the fracas,
the monster guy ripped in half
a brown paper bag
belonging to the kid.
Soon the ride ended.
'I've lost me lunch!'
the kid exclaimed
as we emerged into daylight.
He held the torn-off top of his bag.
But he wasn't unhappy;
in fact, he was grinning
– he'd grappled with a monster,
and emerged unbowed,
undefeated.

Night Journey

What is that sound
of rolling wheels
in the still of night?

Not a freight train,
but kids on skateboards
going home.

The Best Times

The best times are so good
you regret they're slipping through your fingers
while you're having them.

John 18:10–11

Hothead St Peter unsheathed his sword
and cut off the high priest's servant's ear.
He gave new meaning to the expression
'putting an ear to the ground'.

Joseph of Arimathea

Here is your typical
entrepreneur:
wealthy, active in society,
a finger in many pies.
This Christ, he thinks,
well yes, I'll give him
a tomb in which to be buried
– what the hell, he can have mine.
Let's have a look
after three days
and see if he's for real;
if so, I'll certainly
back him to the hilt.
Might even tour him overseas,
help the guy spread his word.

Thailand Silk

Mum's friend 'Pinhead'
fought in the Vietnam War.
He bought her a pure silk scarf in Thailand.
The scarf came back. He didn't.

Murray Cod

Men building the early bridges
across the River Murray
caught Murray cod
off half-finished structures
with fencing wire.
Some fish were enormous,
bigger than the blokes who hooked them.
Old photos from newspapers
of Riverina country towns
and stuffed specimens
above the bars of riverside pubs
tell vivid tales
of men and mythic monster.
These days, though, the big Murray cod
are more elusive than ever.
Locks, weirs and barrages
put across the river,
as well as other
human interventions,
mean the fish have little chance
of growing to their former giant size.
But I cannot help but wonder if,
in quiet backwaters,
dappled with shade and lazy sun,
some fish of mythological
proportions remain,
log-heavy, somnolent relics,
one day to rouse
from the quietude of ages.

Goodbye Georgie

in memoriam George Best 1946–2005

Football genius, womaniser,
hopelessly alcoholic,
charming, charismatic George Best
often told a story
that went something like this:
he was lying on a kingsize bed
next to a half-naked Miss World
in the suite of a grand hotel.
They were drinking French champagne, laughing,
and the bed was covered in money.
An elderly Northern Irish porter
(fellow countryman of George)
chanced upon the scene.
He sadly shook his head.
'George, George,' he lamented.
'Where did it all go wrong?'

Resumé

You know the resumé thing,
when you don't lie, but overstate
the importance of your achievements
– jobs, publications and the like
appear on paper
as more impressive than they actually were?
Take my multi-talented friend.
He put in a theatre program
that he had 'worked in all mediums.'
All mediums?
Really?
It's been a running joke between us since.
Yesterday I phoned him and said,
'Hello, "worker-in-all-mediums".
Done any equestrian statues today?'
I laughed and could hear
his half-hearted chuckle
on the other end of the line.

Zombies

When the dead return,
they're naked.
(No they're not,
but I knew saying that
would attract your attention.)

When the dead return…
they're boring.
Just stand at your bedside
when you're asleep,
or in corners of rooms,
or pin-drop off balconies
of tall buildings.

When the dead return,
they show
no imagination.

Nineteenth Century Street Scene: Evening

Gaslit Paris!
Violet dusk.
Man in top hat, with cane,
accompanies a woman
in a long white dress
with ruffled sleeves.
She holds a parasol,
and leads a curly terrier.
They cross the rainswept street.
A horse-drawn carriage approaches.
On the nearby corner, a girl,
blue ribbons in blonde hair,
sells pink and purple flowers.
Paris!
Gaslit Paris!

My gaze turned
from this picture on the wall
when the lady pizza deliverer
knocked on my motel room door.

Contemplation upon the Death Mask of Alban Berg (1885–1935)

Alban Berg,
in death, looks
deeply sensitive,
eyes closed as if reflecting
upon his final work,
a concerto for violin
composed for a young lady
who died from polio at age eighteen.
He loved this young woman, Manon,
from the time she was born
as if she were his own daughter.
Hence, unsurprisingly wonderful
the concerto's dedication:
'To the memory of an angel'.

The End

I know what the worst time will be
– when I walk out our front door,
away from you,
for the last time.
I'll give our beloved cat
a final play and pat
then he'll trot out to the gate post to wait,
believing I'm coming home again.

www.ingramcontent.com/pod-product-compliance
Lightning Source LLC
Chambersburg PA
CBHW071034080526
44587CB00015B/2615